D1116496

ROOTS ARE
FOOD FINDERS

ROOTS ARE
FOOD FINDERS

By Franklyn M. Branley

Illustrated by Joseph Low

THOMAS Y. CROWELL COMPANY / NEW YORK

LET'S-READ-AND-FIND-OUT SCIENCE BOOKS

Editors: *DR. ROMA GANS*, Professor Emeritus of Childhood Education, Teachers College, Columbia University
DR. FRANKLYN M. BRANLEY, Astronomer Emeritus and former Chairman of The American Museum-Hayden Planetarium

LIVING THINGS: PLANTS

Down Come the Leaves
How a Seed Grows
Mushrooms and Molds
Plants in Winter
Roots Are Food Finders
Seeds by Wind and Water
The Sunlit Sea
A Tree Is a Plant
Water Plants
Where Does Your Garden Grow?

LIVING THINGS: ANIMALS, BIRDS, FISH, INSECTS, ETC.

Animals in Winter
Bats in the Dark
Bees and Beelines
Big Tracks, Little Tracks
Birds at Night
Birds Eat and Eat and Eat
Bird Talk
The Blue Whale
Camels: Ships of the Desert
Cockroaches: Here, There, and Everywhere
Ducks Don't Get Wet
*Available in Spanish

The Emperor Penguins
Fireflies in the Night
Giraffes at Home
Green Grass and White Milk
Green Turtle Mysteries
Hummingbirds in the Garden
Hungry Sharks
It's Nesting Time
Ladybug, Ladybug, Fly Away Home
The Long-Lost Coelacanth and Other Living Fossils
My Daddy Longlegs
My Visit to the Dinosaurs
The Opossum
Peepers in the Spring
Sandpipers
Shrimps
Spider Silk
Spring Peepers
Starfish
Twist, Wiggle, and Squirm: A Book About Earthworms
Watch Honeybees with Me
What I Like About Toads
Why Frogs Are Wet

THE HUMAN BODY

A Baby Starts to Grow
Before You Were a Baby
A Drop of Blood
Fat and Skinny
Find Out by Touching
Follow Your Nose
Hear Your Heart
How Many Teeth?
How You Talk
In the Night
*Look at Your Eyes**
My Five Senses
My Hands
The Skeleton Inside You
Sleep Is for Everyone
*Straight Hair, Curly Hair**
Use Your Brain
What Happens to a Hamburger
*Your Skin and Mine**

And other books on AIR, WATER, AND WEATHER; THE EARTH AND ITS COMPOSITION; ASTRONOMY AND SPACE; and MATTER AND ENERGY

Copyright © 1975 by Franklyn M. Branley. Illustrations copyright © 1975 by Joseph Low. All rights reserved. Except for use in a review, the reproduction or utilization of this work in any form or by any electronic, mechanical, or other means, now known or hereafter invented, including xerography, photocopying, and recording, and in any information storage and retrieval system is forbidden without the written permission of the publisher. Published simultaneously in Canada by Fitzhenry & Whiteside Limited, Toronto. Manufactured in the United States of America.

Library of Congress Cataloging in Publication Data Branley, Franklyn Mansfield, 1915-   Roots are food finders. SUMMARY: Explains in simple terms the function and importance of roots and root hairs on a plant.   1. Roots (Botany)—Juvenile literature. [1. Roots (Botany) 2. Plants]   I. Low, Joseph, 1911- illus. II. Title. QK644.B65 582′.01′3   74-23924   ISBN 0-690-00702-7   ISBN 0-690-00703-5 lib. bdg.

1   2   3   4   5   6   7   8   9   10

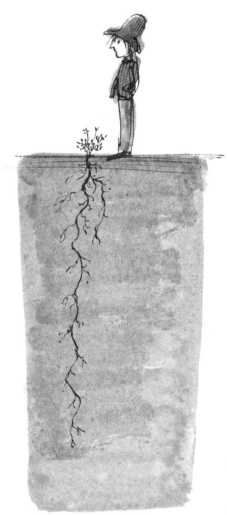

LET'S READ AND FIND OUT

ROOTS ARE FOOD FINDERS

You have hair on your head.

Dogs and cats and
lots of other animals
have hair.

Plants have hair, too.

Plants don't have real hair.
But something that looks like hair
grows on plant roots.

Root hairs are as thin
as the hair on your head—so
thin you can hardly see them.

1

In order to grow,
plants must have water,
just as we must.

They need air too, just as we do.

Plants also need minerals.
Calcium,
     phosphorus,
        sulfur,
          chlorine,
            and magnesium
are some of the minerals that plants need.

We need these minerals, too.

Plants

and animals

and people

need minerals to stay healthy
and to grow.

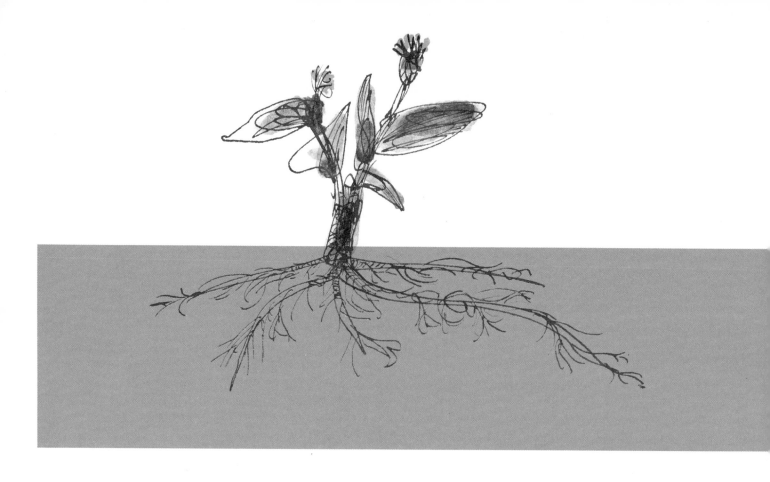

Plants get their minerals from the soil.
They get them through their roots
and their very small root hairs.

Animals and people cannot get minerals the way plants do. They get some of the minerals that they need from the water that they drink.

But they get most of their minerals by eating the plants that grow in the soil.

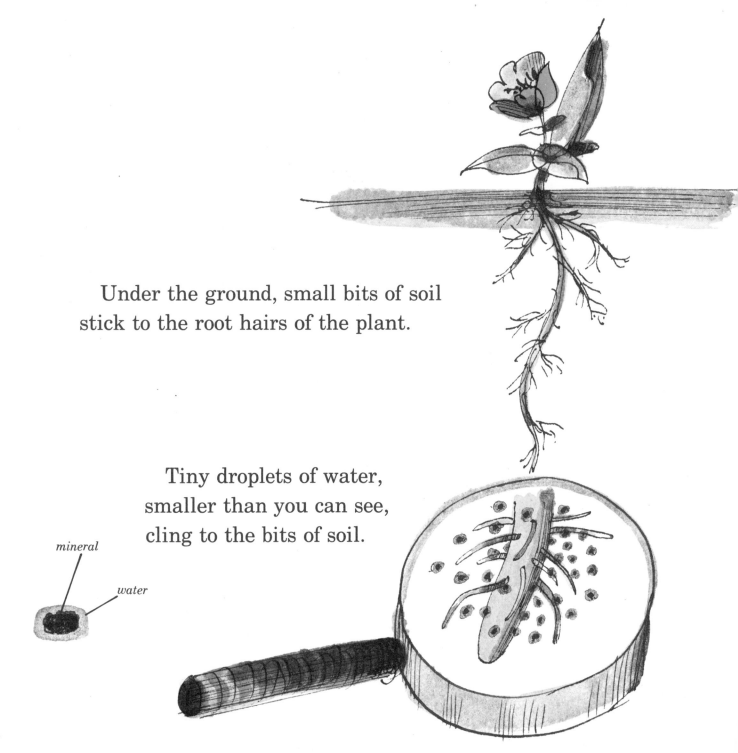

Under the ground, small bits of soil
stick to the root hairs of the plant.

Tiny droplets of water,
smaller than you can see,
cling to the bits of soil.

mineral

water

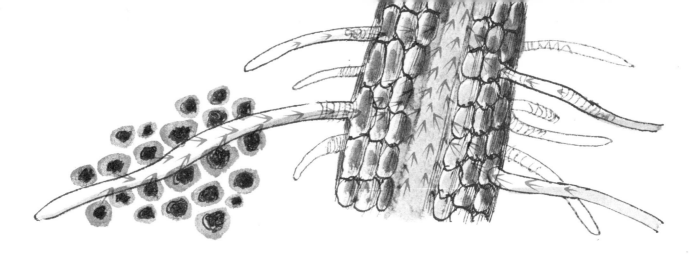

This water, with minerals in it, goes right through
the walls of the root hairs and into the plant.
Plants are mineral collectors. They store the
minerals that they collect in their roots, stems,
and leaves.

If plants did not have roots and tiny root hairs,
they could not gather minerals. If plants did not
get minerals from the soil, they would not grow.
Then there would be no food for animals or for
people. So roots and root hairs are very important.

You can see root hairs on seeds
after they start to grow.

Put radish seeds and grass seeds
in a jar of water
and soak them overnight.

If you have soybeans, mung beans, lentils,
or whole peas, put some of them in the jar too.
You'll use them later on.

The next day put a single layer
of cheesecloth over the mouth of the jar.

Hold it in place with a rubber band.

Drain off the water.

Fill the jar with fresh water,
and swish it around
to rinse the seeds.

Then drain off the water.

Lay the jar on its side in a dark closet.

Rinse the seeds the same way
three or four times a day.

After two or three days
the seeds will start to grow.
Some seeds grow faster than others.

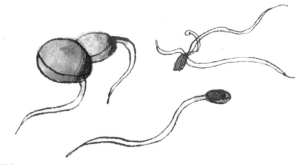

You will see roots coming out of them.
The roots are white.
    In four or five days leaves will start to grow
and the roots will be much bigger.
    They are fat at the top
and pointed at the bottom.

Give the roots time to grow.

Soon, little roots
will grow out of them.
Look at these
through a magnifying glass.

Tiny root hairs will grow at the ends of the little roots.
They're easy to see
on the mung bean roots.

Suppose you could look under the ground and
see the roots of an apple tree. Just under the ground,
the main root becomes many smaller roots.

Even smaller roots grow out of each of these roots.

The roots grow deep into the ground. There
is almost as much tree under the ground as there
is above the ground.

At the ends of the small roots
there are root hairs.

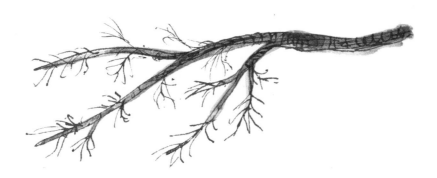

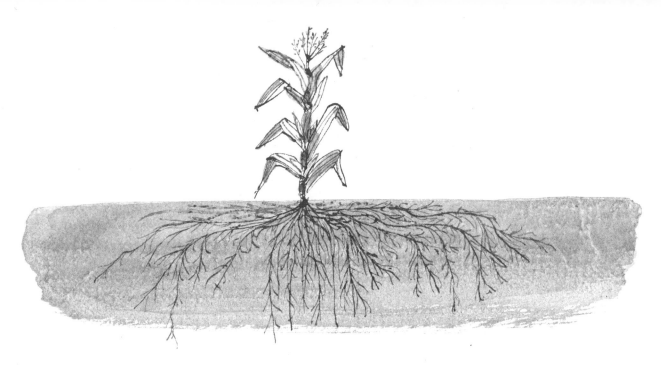

The roots of a corn plant are different from those of an apple tree. They begin about an inch under the ground and spread out wide, instead of down.

Suppose you are four feet tall. If you were to lie on the ground with your head touching a corn plant, your feet would be just about over the ends of the roots. That's how far out the roots spread. A corn plant has hundreds of roots, and each root has root hairs near the end of it.

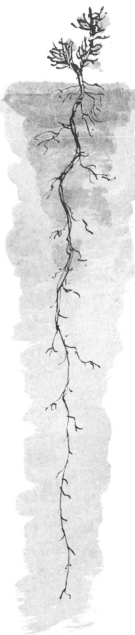

The roots of all plants gather minerals
and water from the soil where they grow.

When the soil is dry, the roots
must spread out farther to get water.

Or they must go deeper into the ground
where the soil has not dried out.

Sometimes not much rain falls in the western part of the United States.

Then the grass gets dry, turns brown, and does not grow well.

A few plants, such as the creosote bush and the locoweed, stay green.

Grass dries out because its roots cannot gather water. They don't go deep enough.

The locoweeds do not dry out. That's because their roots go down very deep, to where there is water. A locoweed may grow as high as your knee. Its roots will go down twice as deep as you are tall. There is one main root, and little roots grow out from it. These small roots gather water and minerals. So do the root hairs. The locoweed gets enough water to stay green even when the weather is very dry.

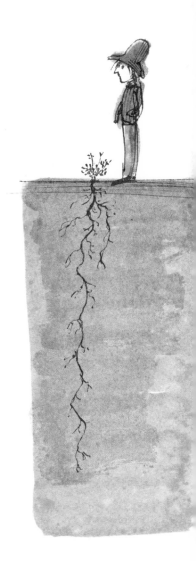

SGS LIBRARY

Some plants live in the desert, where it doesn't rain very much, but their roots don't go deep into the ground.

One of these plants is the prickly pear cactus.

It is a small plant, only a few inches high.

Its roots grow only three or four inches down into the ground.

But they spread out far enough to cover a space as big as a Ping-Pong table.

18

It rains only once in a while
where the prickly pear grows.
 When it does rain, the rain goes
only a few inches into the ground.

 But that's deep enough to reach the roots
of the prickly pear.
 Water and minerals are collected by the root hairs
and stored in the roots and in the stem.
 During dry weather, the prickly pear
uses the stored water and minerals.

Probably there will be another sprinkle of rain before the plant's supply is gone.

Once more the shallow roots will gather water and minerals.

Sometimes travelers in the desert cut open the top of a barrel cactus to squeeze out a life-giving drink of water.

You have seen small roots and root hairs on the
seeds that you sprouted. Now you can watch your
small plants grow bigger.

You will need a glass and a piece of cardboard
a little bigger than the glass.

With a sharp pencil poke three or four holes
through the cardboard.

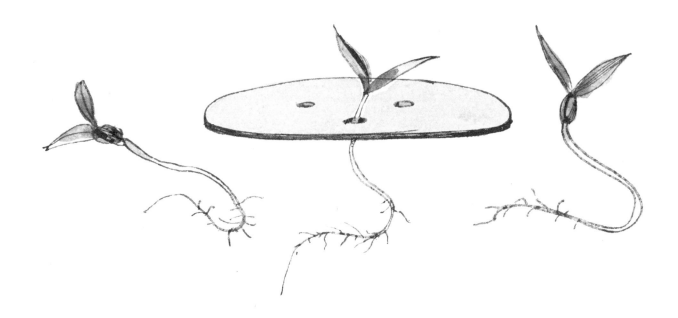

Put one of your seed sprouts through each hole, root first.

Use the bean sprouts, or the lentil sprouts.

Be careful you do not break the roots.

Fill the glass with water
and place the cardboard over it.

Wrap aluminum foil around the glass
to keep out the light.

The roots will be in the water
and in the dark.

The small leaves will be on the outside.

Place the glass where it will be in the light.

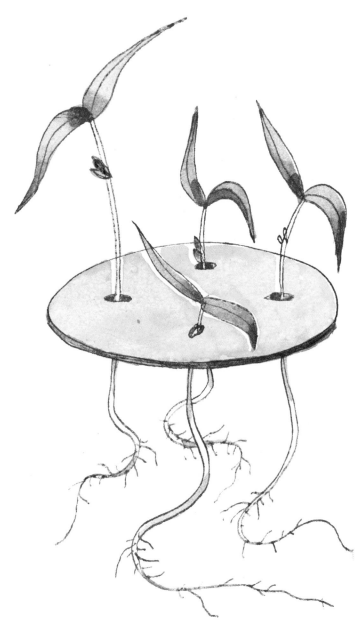

In a day or two
the sprouts will grow a lot.

The roots will be longer
and the leaves will be larger.

When your seeds have grown
you might want more new roots,
to experiment with them.

After the plants are growing well—
that should be in three or four days—
lift off the cardboard and the plants.

Put ten drops or more of red vegetable dye into the water,
and put back the cardboard.

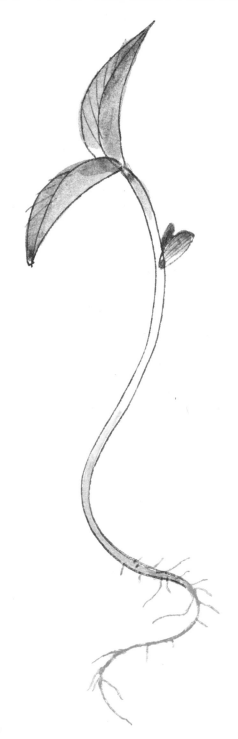

After two or three days
see if the color has gone
into the roots.

Maybe the roots will become reddish.

Maybe the stems will too.

Sometimes some of the dye
even reaches the leaves.

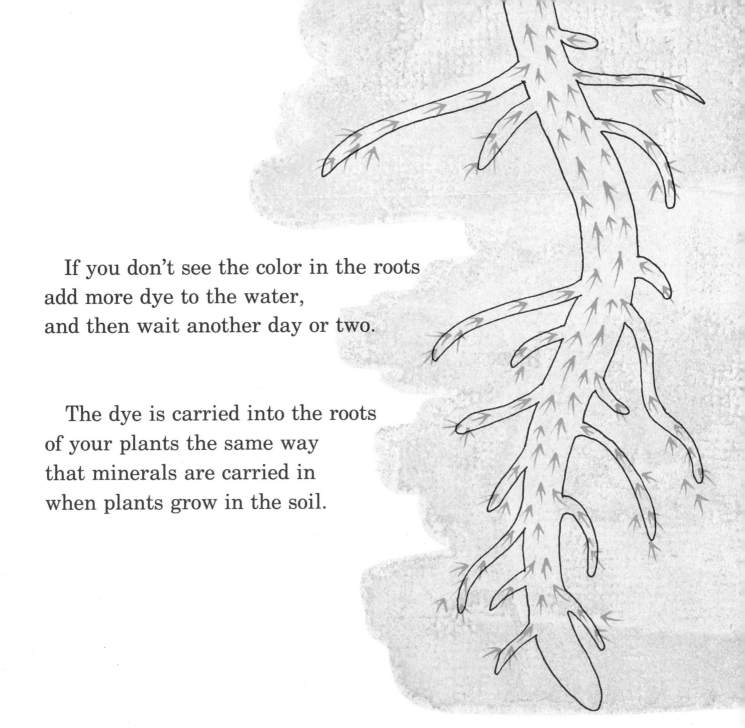

If you don't see the color in the roots
add more dye to the water,
and then wait another day or two.

The dye is carried into the roots
of your plants the same way
that minerals are carried in
when plants grow in the soil.

When you see plants
pulled out of the ground—
flowers,
　　　bushes,
　　　　　great big trees—
look at the roots.

Notice that some are big,
and others are much smaller.

At the ends of the small ones
there may still be some root
hairs that were not rubbed off.
But remember, they are very
small, so small you can hardly
see them.

Pull up a dandelion and see
how long its root is.

All plants have root hairs.

Some have many more than others.

Once a scientist grew a rye plant
in a box.

Rye is like a tall grass.

When he dug up the plant,
he washed the soil off the roots.

Then he measured
the length of each root.
All together they added up
to 387 miles. When the root hairs
were measured, they added up
to 7000 miles!

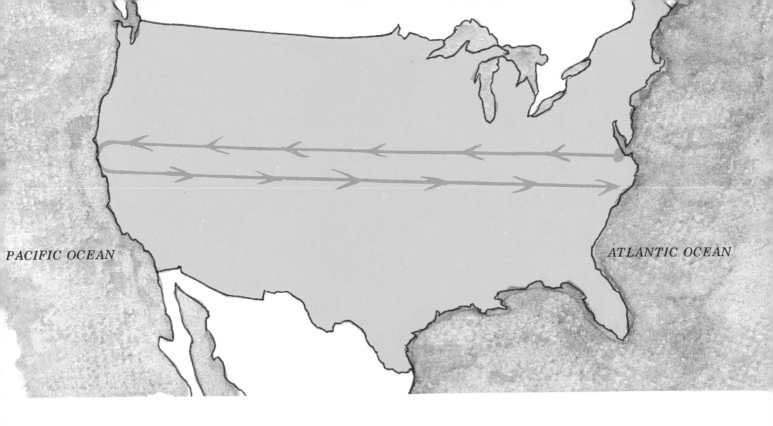

PACIFIC OCEAN

ATLANTIC OCEAN

That's enough to go all the way from the Atlantic
Ocean to the Pacific Ocean and back again.

And all these were on just one plant!

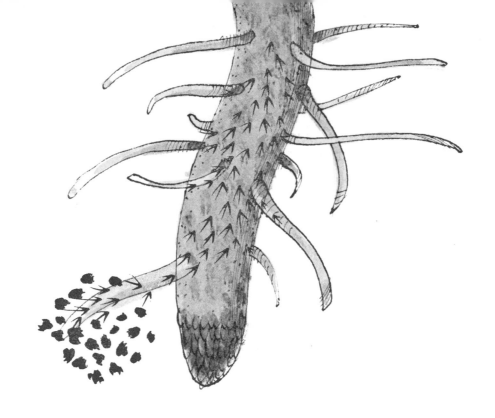

Every plant has lots of tiny root hairs.
They are very important.

Roots and root hairs collect minerals
from the soil and store them in plants.

Without minerals, plants could not live.

And neither could anything else.

All living things need minerals to grow. They get them from plants.

Roots and root hairs are mineral collectors. They are food finders.

About the Author

Franklyn M. Branley, Astronomer Emeritus and former Chairman of The American Museum–Hayden Planetarium, is well known as the author of many books about science for young people of all ages. He is also coeditor of the Let's-Read-and-Find-Out Science Books.

Dr. Branley holds degrees from New York University, Columbia University, and the State University of New York College at New Paltz. He and his wife live in Woodcliff Lake, New Jersey.

About the Illustrator

Joseph Low was born in a small river town near Pittsburgh, grew up in Illinois, studied at that state's university and at the Art Students League in New York. He taught for a few years at Indiana University, then left to free-lance in New York, living in the countryside rather than in the city itself. For a time, with his Eden Hill Press, he became a printer and publisher as well as an artist. His work has been exhibited and collected by museums across the United States, in Europe, South America, and the Orient. Mr. Low and his wife now divide their year between two islands: Martha's Vineyard for summers in the north; St. John for winters in the Caribbean. In both he is able to indulge a passion for sailing.

SGS LIBRARY